Invisible Journeys
Sun

CREATIVE AND EDITORIAL DIRECTOR
CONCEPT/FORMAT/DESIGN/TEXT

CAROLINE GRIMSHAW

TEXT EDITOR

IQBAL HUSSAIN

SCIENCE CONSULTANT

JOHN STRINGER UNIVERSITY OF WARWICK, U.K.

ILLUSTRATIONS

NICK DUFFY ※ SPIKE GERRELL

CAROLINE GRIMSHAW

THANKS TO

PATRICIA OHLENROTH, WORLD BOOK, INC.

TITLES IN THIS SERIES ---→ ※ SUN
※ COMMUNICATION

FIRST PUBLISHED IN THE UNITED STATES AND CANADA BY
WORLD BOOK, INC., 525 W. MONROE, CHICAGO, IL 60661
IN ASSOCIATION WITH TWO-CAN PUBLISHING LTD.
COPYRIGHT © CAROLINE GRIMSHAW/ 1997.

FOR INFORMATION ON OTHER WORLD BOOK PRODUCTS,
CALL 1-800-255-1750, X 2238, OR VISIT US AT OUR WEB SITE AT
HTTP://WWW.WORLDBOOK.COM

GRIMSHAW, CAROLINE
SUN/CAROLINE GRIMSHAW.
P. CM. -- (INVISIBLE JOURNEYS)
INCLUDES INDEX.
SUMMARY; QUESTIONS AND ANSWERS EXPLORE THE MOVEMENT, ENERGY, AND
INFLUENCES OF THE SUN.
ISBN: 0-7166-3003-6 (PBK.)   ISBN: 0-7166-3002-8 (HBK.)
1. SUN--MISCELLANEA--JUVENILE LITERATURE. [1. SUN--MISCELLANEA.
2. QUESTIONS AND ANSWERS.] I. TITLE. II. SERIES.
QB521.5.G75 1997
523.7--DC21   97-22072

PRINTED IN HONG KONG
1 2 3 4 5 6 7 8 9 10 01 00 99 98 97

Safety Note Never look directly at the sun, even through sunglasses. And never, ever look at the sun with binoculars or a telescope. Whenever you are out in the hot sun, protect yourself by putting on sun screen and wearing a wide-brimmed hat.

I am your Route Scout. I will be with you on your journey. Look for my two companions.

Welcome
TO
Invisible Journeys

THE Highway

Travel along the *Highway* following a sunbeam's journey from its source (the Sun) to its end (the Earth).

THE Side Roads

On your journey, you will be asked to select your own route. Choose a side road and follow its route.

THE Road Stops

The Side Roads lead you to Road Stops, which contain vital information about your trip. These may lead you farther on to the Points of Interest, which are bursting with more fascinating facts. Visible Proof Spots will test your knowledge with experiments and puzzles. Detours allow you to leap forward to Road Stops farther along the route. They have a symbol that looks like this. ------------------------→

Let's head for Earth!

Detour

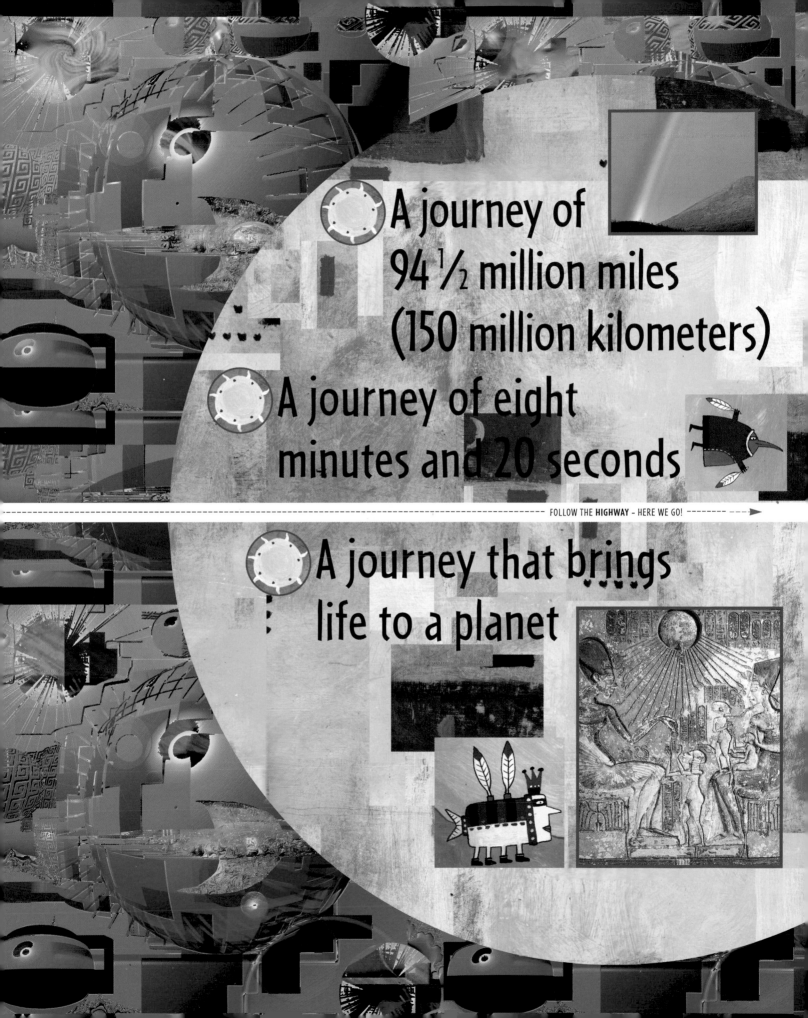

A journey of 94 ½ million miles (150 million kilometers)

A journey of eight minutes and 20 seconds

A journey that brings life to a planet

The source of all sunbeams is the sun.

Beware! Look out for solar winds and giant flares.

FOLLOW THE **HIGHWAY**. ┄┄┄┄┄┄┄┄┄┄┄┄┄┄►

This is where our journey starts – 94 ½ million miles (150 million kilometers) from Earth.

The visible surface of the sun is called the **PHOTOSPHERE**. It has a temperature of 10,000 °F (5,500 °C). It contains small patches of gas called **GRANULES** that fade away after 5 to 10 minutes and are then replaced by new ones.

The Sun is a star. Let's examine this star in more detail.

Select
YOUR SIDE ROAD

The sun

1 What's it made of?
(AND WHAT'S INSIDE OF IT?)

2 How big is it?

3 How old is it?
(AND HOW WAS IT BORN?)

4 How hot is it?
(AND WHAT MAKES IT SHINE?)

5 What is the the sun's place in the universe?
(AND WILL THE SUN LAST FOREVER?)

6 Does the Sun move?
(AND WHAT IS AN ECLIPSE?)

SIDE ROAD TO ROAD STOP

SIDE ROAD TO ROAD STOP

SIDE ROAD TO ROAD STOP

SIDE ROAD TO ROAD STOP

SIDE ROAD TO ROAD STOP

SIDE ROAD TO ROAD STOP

ROAD STOP

1

What's the sun made of?

The sun is a huge glowing ball of hot gases. It is made up almost entirely of two gases called hydrogen and helium.

How do we know this? Scientists have studied the pattern of colored lines that make up sunlight. This pattern is called a spectrum. From this spectrum, scientists can determine which chemicals are in the sun.

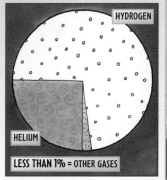

HYDROGEN

HELIUM

LESS THAN 1% = OTHER GASES

ABOUT 75% = HYDROGEN This is the lightest and simplest gas known. Hydrogen is vital for various processes that go on in the human body and is also used as a fuel in industry.

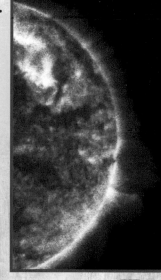

ABOUT 25% = HELIUM Scientists discovered this gas on the sun before they found it on Earth. The name comes from the Greek "helios" meaning "sun." As it is lighter than air and will not burn like hydrogen, helium is used in scientific balloons. It is also used to help people with breathing difficulties.

LET'S JOURNEY TO THE CENTER OF THE SUN. FOLLOW THE PATH TO THE **POINT OF INTEREST.**

← ROAD STOP 1 →

ROAD STOP 2 →

ROAD STOP

2

How big is the sun?

The diameter is 865,000 miles (1,392,000 km).

The sun is in a group of stars astronomers call **YELLOW DWARVES**. Compared with other stars, it is only medium-sized. Stars called **SUPERGIANTS** have a diameter 1,000 times that of the sun.

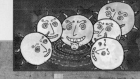

DOES THE SUN CHANGE SIZE? Only very slightly as it pulsates. In warm countries, the sun may appear bigger because the Earth's atmosphere magnifies our view of the sun when it is setting.

Visible Proof **SPOT**

Imagine that the sun's diameter is the height of an adult. Jupiter, the largest planet in the solar system, is the size of the head, and Earth smaller than the eyeball. The sun is so huge you could fit a million balls the size of the Earth inside it.

5

POINT of Interest

Let's open up the sun and take a look inside.

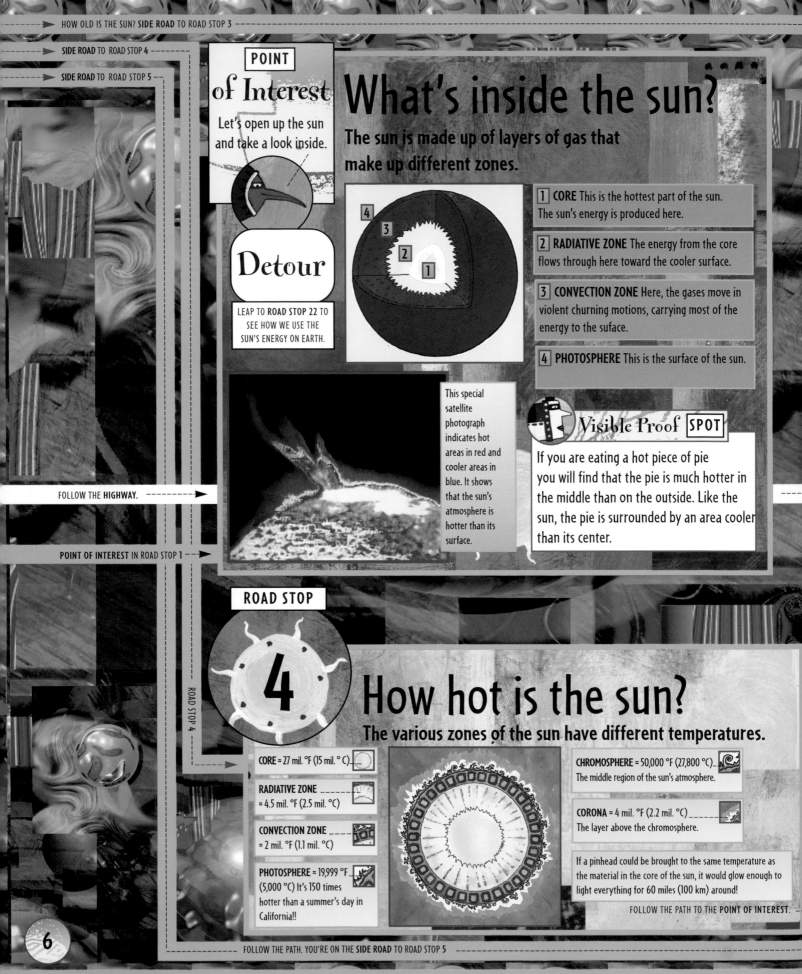

Detour

LEAP TO **ROAD STOP 22** TO SEE HOW WE USE THE SUN'S ENERGY ON EARTH.

FOLLOW THE **HIGHWAY.**

POINT OF INTEREST IN ROAD STOP 1

What's inside the sun?

The sun is made up of layers of gas that make up different zones.

1 **CORE** This is the hottest part of the sun. The sun's energy is produced here.

2 **RADIATIVE ZONE** The energy from the core flows through here toward the cooler surface.

3 **CONVECTION ZONE** Here, the gases move in violent churning motions, carrying most of the energy to the suface.

4 **PHOTOSPHERE** This is the surface of the sun.

This special satellite photograph indicates hot areas in red and cooler areas in blue. It shows that the sun's atmosphere is hotter than its surface.

Visible Proof SPOT

If you are eating a hot piece of pie you will find that the pie is much hotter in the middle than on the outside. Like the sun, the pie is surrounded by an area cooler than its center.

ROAD STOP

4

How hot is the sun?

The various zones of the sun have different temperatures.

CORE = 27 mil. °F (15 mil. ° C)

RADIATIVE ZONE = 4.5 mil. °F (2.5 mil. °C)

CONVECTION ZONE = 2 mil. °F (1.1 mil. °C)

PHOTOSPHERE = 19,999 °F (5,000 °C) It's 150 times hotter than a summer's day in California!!

CHROMOSPHERE = 50,000 °F (27,800 °C) The middle region of the sun's atmosphere.

CORONA = 4 mil. °F (2.2 mil. °C) The layer above the chromosphere.

If a pinhead could be brought to the same temperature as the material in the core of the sun, it would glow enough to light everything for 60 miles (100 km) around!

FOLLOW THE PATH TO THE **POINT OF INTEREST.**

ROAD STOP

3

How old is the sun?

The sun is about 4,600 million years old! This is ...

10 times as old as the first land plants.

2,300 times as old as the human race.

Detour

LEAP TO **ROAD STOP 24** TO LOOK AT THE CHANGING THEORIES OF THE PEOPLE WHO HAVE STUDIED THE SUN.

39 million times as old as the oldest human being in the world.

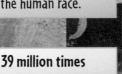

How do we know this? Scientists have studied meteorites–rocks from space–and moon rocks that were created at the same time as the sun. These rocks give off radiation. The amount of radiation they give off helps scientists determine their age.

FOLLOW THE PATH TO THE POINT OF INTEREST.

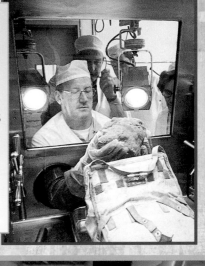

FOLLOW THE **HIGHWAY** TO INVESTIGATE A SUNBEAM. ⟶

POINT of Interest

Does heat and energy make the sun shine?

What makes the sun shine?

A chemical reaction in the sun's core.

Detour

WILL THE SUN SHINE FOREVER? TO FIND OUT LEAP TO **ROAD STOP 5**.

Hydrogen gas changes to helium, creating energy that travels through to the photosphere, where it leaves the sun as heat and light. This causes the sun to shine.

Sometimes, there is a small, bright burst on the sun called a flare. It is caused by eruptions of gases on the sun's surface. Flares can produce a jet of flaming gas thousands of miles high.

POINT of Interest

Did the sun just appear one day?

How was it born?

This is what people think happened.

The sun is a star. Stars are formed when gases and dust join together and begin to contract under the force of gravity. This produces more and more heat until chemical reactions take place that cause the gases and dust to shine as a star.

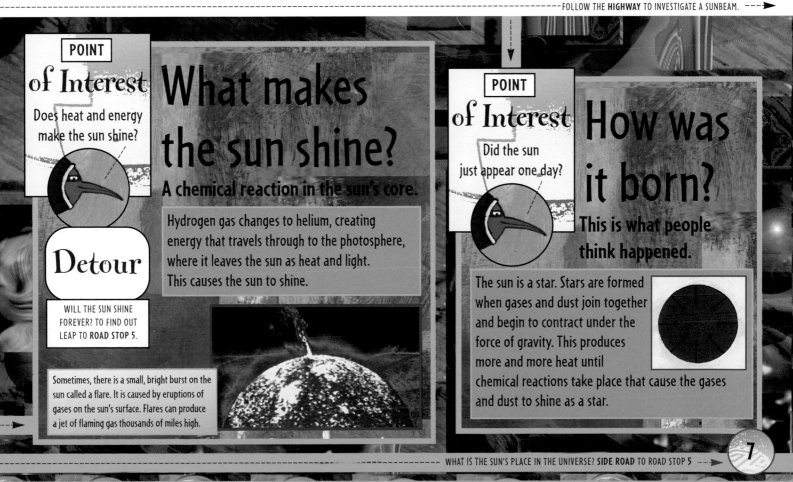

WHAT IS THE SUN'S PLACE IN THE UNIVERSE? **SIDE ROAD** TO ROAD STOP 5

DOES THE SUN MOVE? **SIDE ROAD** TO ROAD STOP 6

5 What is the sun's place in the universe?

The sun is one star in a group of hundreds of billions of stars that form our galaxy. We call our galaxy the Milky Way.

What is the solar system?

The sun is at the center of our solar system. There are nine planets, including the Earth, that orbit the sun.

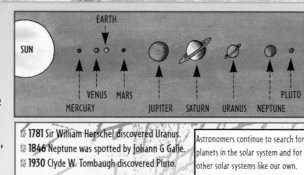

EARTH

SUN

MERCURY · VENUS · MARS · JUPITER · SATURN · URANUS · NEPTUNE · PLUTO

※ **1781** Sir William Herschel discovered Uranus.
※ **1846** Neptune was spotted by Johann G Galle.
※ **1930** Clyde W. Tombaugh discovered Pluto.

Astronomers continue to search for planets in the solar system and for other solar systems like our own.

Detour

LEAP TO **ROAD STOP 21** TO FIND OUT HOW WE USE THE SUN TO RECORD OUR WORLD.

PLANET	DIAMETER MILES (KM)	DISTANCE FROM SUN MIL. MILES (MIL. KM)	TIME TAKEN TO ORBIT THE SUN
MERCURY	3,031 (4,878)	35.9 (57.9)	87.97 EARTH DAYS
VENUS	7,521 (12,104)	67.2 (108.2)	224.7 EARTH DAYS
EARTH	7,926 (12,756)	92.9 (149.6)	365.26 EARTH DAYS
MARS	4,223 (6,796)	141 (227.9)	686.98 EARTH DAYS
JUPITER	88,846 (142,984)	483.6 (778.4)	4,332.7 EARTH YEARS
SATURN	74,898 (120,536)	888.2 (1,427)	10,759 EARTH YEARS
URANUS	31,763 (51,118)	1,786.4 (2,875)	30,685 EARTH YEARS
NEPTUNE	30,800 (49,500)	2,798.8 (4,504)	60,190 EARTH YEARS
PLUTO	1,430 (2,300)	3,666.2 (5,900)	90,800 EARTH YEARS

→ FOLLOW THE **HIGHWAY**.

- - → WILL THE SUN BE AROUND FOREVER?

6 Does the sun move?

The sun spins on its axis and also revolves around the center of the galaxy.

Compare the Earth and the sun.

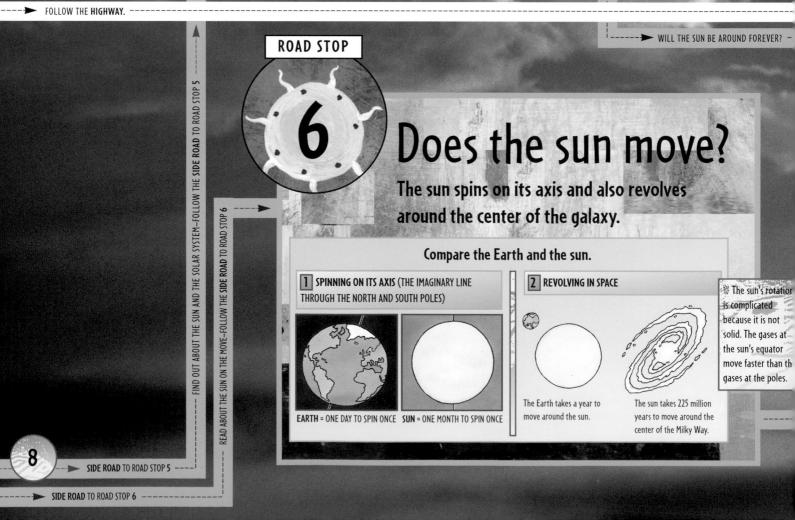

1 SPINNING ON ITS AXIS (THE IMAGINARY LINE THROUGH THE NORTH AND SOUTH POLES)

EARTH = ONE DAY TO SPIN ONCE   **SUN = ONE MONTH TO SPIN ONCE**

2 REVOLVING IN SPACE

The Earth takes a year to move around the sun.

The sun takes 225 million years to move around the center of the Milky Way.

※ The sun's rotation is complicated because it is not solid. The gases at the sun's equator move faster than the gases at the poles.

↑ FIND OUT ABOUT THE SUN AND THE SOLAR SYSTEM—FOLLOW THE SIDE ROAD TO ROAD STOP 5

↑ READ ABOUT THE SUN ON THE MOVE—FOLLOW THE SIDE ROAD TO ROAD STOP 6

FOLLOW THIS ROUTE TO THE **POINT OF INTEREST.**

POINT

of Interest

Can the sun really die?

Will the sun last forever?

Our star will probably die one day. Scientists predict that the sun will shine for at least another 5 billion years.

This is what may happen.

1 FAST FORWARD TO 5,000,000,000 YEARS TIME
❋ **TEMPERATURE** The center of the sun shrinks and gets hotter. The surface temperature will fall slightly.
❋ **ENERGY** Because of the heat at the center, the sun gives off more energy.
❋ **SIZE** The sun expands by billions of miles (or kilometers), stretching out as far as Mercury.

2 The sun is now a **RED GIANT STAR**. The sun is too hot for life to exist on Earth.

3 The sun now shrinks to the size of the Earth and becomes a **WHITE DWARF**.

4 Billions of years later the sun has used up its energy and lost its heat. It is now a **BLACK DWARF**—a cold, dark globe. Earth is now freezing cold.

How do we know this? Astronomers look at stars that are older than the sun and watch them go through this process.

This picture shows the corona—the outer edge of the sun's atmosphere.

Detour

SEE HOW THE SUN GIVES LIFE TO PLANET EARTH. LEAP TO ROAD STOP 13.

FOLLOW THE **HIGHWAY** TO FIND OUT ABOUT LIGHT.

FOLLOW THIS ROUTE TO THE **POINT OF INTEREST.**

POINT

of Interest

When is the sun hidden?

What is an eclipse?

The Earth and moon are constantly moving around the sun. From Earth, the sun and moon appear to be the same size. As a result, when the moon lies between the Earth and the sun, it can block out the sun completely. A shadow is cast on the Earth. We call this event an eclipse.

Detour

LEAP TO **ROAD STOP 19** TO SEE HOW THE SUN HAS INFLUENCED WHAT PEOPLE BELIEVE.

Visible Proof SPOT

Shine a flashlight on an apple. The light is the sunlight and the apple is the Earth. For the moon, put a small ball of clay on the end of a metal wire. Place the moon between the Earth and the sun and watch as parts of the Earth experience a total eclipse.

Depending on where you are on the Earth, the eclipse may be total or partial. A **TOTAL ECLIPSE** happens if the moon completely blots out the sun. When the moon covers only a part of the sun, a **PARTIAL ECLIPSE** happens.

SUNLIGHT   SHADOW EARTH

SUN

TOTAL ECLIPSE VIEWED HERE.

MOON

During a total eclipse scientists can study the glowing gases around the sun.

WHEN DOES THE SUN DISAPPEAR FROM THE SKY? FOLLOW THIS ROUTE TO THE **POINT OF INTEREST.**

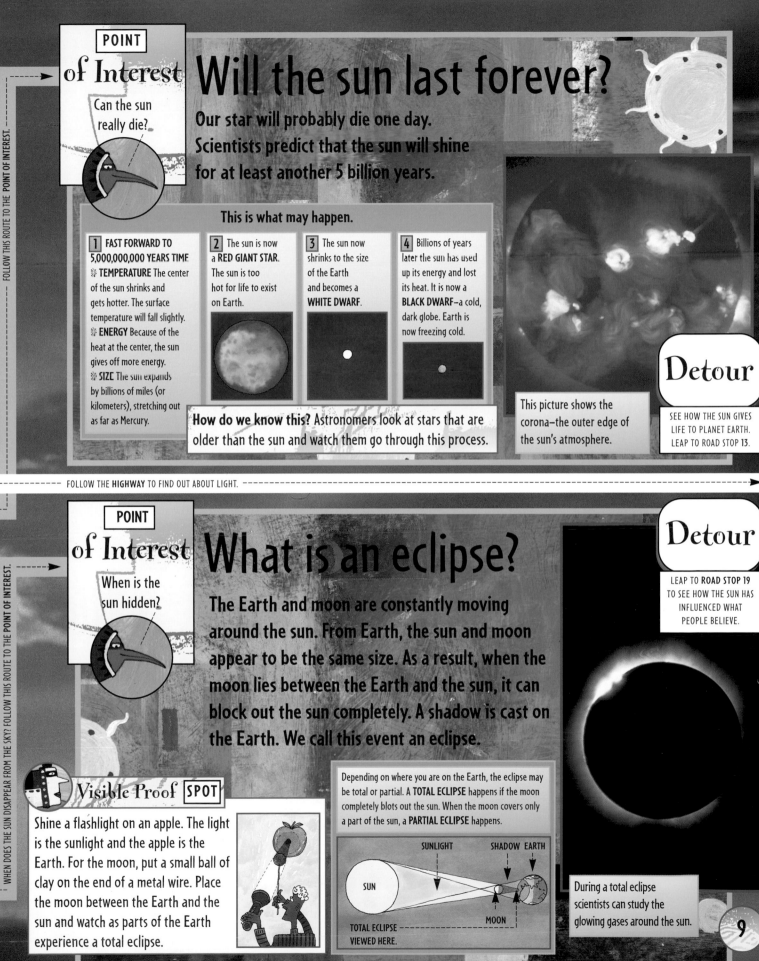

Let's take a look at rays of light.

Select
YOUR SIDE ROAD

Sunbeams

7 Who first studied light? (AND WHAT EXACTLY IS IT?) ----- → SIDE ROAD TO ROAD STOP 7

8 What color is sunlight? (AND ARE ALL OF THE SUN'S RAYS VISIBLE?)

9 How fast do sunbeams travel? ----- → SIDE ROAD TO ROAD STOP 9

10 Do all sunbeams reach the Earth? ----- → SIDE ROAD TO ROAD STOP 10

Whoosh!
What is the speed of light? How can you look back in time?

SIDE ROAD TO ROAD STOP 8

FOLLOW THE **HIGHWAY.** YOU ARE ON THE JOURNEY THAT BRINGS LIFE TO A PLANET. -----

---

ROAD STOP

7

Who first studied light?

People once thought that light was a ray that traveled from the eye to an object and then back to the eye. Then, in 1666, two men found out more about light.

Detour

LEAP TO **ROAD STOP 11** TO FIND OUT MORE ABOUT LIGHT AND COLOR.

1 In 1666, the English scientist **ISAAC NEWTON** discovered that light could be separated into a wide range of colors. He suggested that light consists of small particles traveling through space.

ROAD STOP

8

What color is sunlight?

We think of sunlight as being white light, but it is actually made up of many different colors.

Visible Proof SPOT

You can see light rays changing direction by doing this simple experiment. Put a colored straw in a glass of water. It seems to bend because light travels more slowly through water.

DO WE KNOW WHAT LIGHT REALLY IS? FOLLOW THE PATH TO THE **POINT OF INTEREST.**

2 At the same time, the Dutch astronomer **CHRISTIAAN HUYGENS** believed that light was made up of waves that traveled at different speeds through different materials. For example, it traveled faster through air than through water. This helped to explain why light could be separated into a spectrum of colors, but not why light traveled in straight lines.

POINT of Interest
Find out about photons

※ If an object gives off light it is said to be luminous. The sun is luminous. Energy is carried from the sun to the Earth by light.

So what exactly is light?

Light is a form of energy that travels through space.

Today, scientists think that neither Newton nor Huygens were completely right. Light is now thought of as small parcels of energy that we call photons, after the Greek word "photos" which means "light."

LIGHT SOMETIMES BEHAVES LIKE PARTICLES.

LIGHT

LIGHT SOMETIMES BEHAVES LIKE WAVES.

Detour
LEAP TO **ROAD STOP 12** TO FIND OUT HOW WE FEEL SUNLIGHT.

FOLLOW THE **HIGHWAY.** ---->

LOOKING AT THE SPECTRUM When light passes through a triangular piece of glass called a prism, it separates into a spectrum of red, orange, yellow, green, blue, indigo, and violet. Newton named the seven colors of the spectrum.

WHITE LIGHT ENTERS PRISM

PRISM SEPARATES THE COLORS BY BENDING THE LIGHT

EACH RAY OF LIGHT IS MADE OF WAVES THAT HAVE DIFFERENT LENGTHS. A WAVELENGTH IS THE DISTANCE FROM THE TOP OF ONE WAVE TO THE TOP OF THE NEXT.

CAN WE SEE ALL OF THE SUN'S RAYS? FOLLOW THE PATH TO THE **POINT OF INTEREST.**

Visible Proof SPOT

Place a white piece of paper on a table in the sunshine. Carefully tilt a clear piece of plastic toward the paper. See how the sunlight separates into the colors of the spectrum.

POINT of Interest
Examine the invisible spectrum

Are all rays visible?

No! The light we see is called "visible light." This is a tiny part of the energy that comes from the sun.

The sun has an invisible spectrum that includes infrared and ultraviolet rays that we cannot see. Ultraviolet rays are named because they lie beyond the violet end of the spectrum.

Detour
SEE HOW TOO MUCH ULTRAVIOLET LIGHT CAN BE HARMFUL. LEAP TO **ROAD STOP 16.**

ROAD STOP

9

How fast do sunbeams travel?

Sunbeams travel at the speed of light.

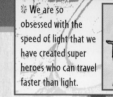

※ We are so obsessed with the speed of light that we have created super heroes who can travel faster than light.

Light travels faster than anything else in the universe. The speed of light is 186,282 miles (299,792 km) per second.

Detour

LEAP TO **ROAD STOP 22** TO SEE HOW WE CAN USE THE POWER OF SUNLIGHT.

Who first tried to measure the speed of light?

1 In the early 1600's, the Italian scientist **GALILEO GALILEI** tried to measure the speed of light by seeing how long it took to see a light that was being switched on at the top of a distant hill. Unfortunately, light travels too fast for people to measure on this small scale.

2 In 1675, the Danish astronomer **OLAUS ROEMER** proved that light travels at a fixed speed. The best estimate he got was 140,430 miles (226,000 km) per second.

3 In 1926, the American physicist **ALBERT MICHELSON** experimented with spinning mirrors to find the speed of light. He measured 186,284 miles (299,796 km) per second–just faster than the real speed.

Visible Proof | SPOT

When you look at the stars, you are really looking back in time! The light you see actually left the stars many years ago.

FOLLOW THE **HIGHWAY** AND FIND OUT ABOUT THE IMPACT OF THE SUN ON OUR PLANET.

SIDE ROAD TO ROAD STOP 9

FOLLOW THE PATH TO FIND OUT ABOUT THE SPEED OF LIGHT.

ROAD STOP

10

Do all sunbeams reach the Earth?

Detour

LEAP TO **ROAD STOP 13** TO SEE HOW THE ATMOSPHERE ALLOWS LIFE TO FLOURISH.

SIDE ROAD TO ROAD STOP 10

Less than half of the sunlight that enters the atmosphere ever reaches the surface of the Earth.

What is the atmosphere? The atmosphere is the layer of gases, water, and dust that surrounds the Earth. It is about 560 miles (900 km) deep, and it protects us from the sun's rays and from pieces of rock called meteorites that fall toward the Earth.

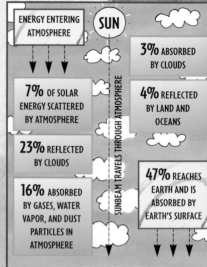

ENERGY ENTERING ATMOSPHERE

SUN

3% ABSORBED BY CLOUDS

7% OF SOLAR ENERGY SCATTERED BY ATMOSPHERE

4% REFLECTED BY LAND AND OCEANS

23% REFLECTED BY CLOUDS

16% ABSORBED BY GASES, WATER VAPOR, AND DUST PARTICLES IN ATMOSPHERE

47% REACHES EARTH AND IS ABSORBED BY EARTH'S SURFACE

SUNBEAM TRAVELS THROUGH ATMOSPHERE

THESE ARE AVERAGE FIGURES. WHEN SKIES ARE CLEAR, ABOUT 80% OF SUNLIGHT REACHES THE EARTH, AND WHEN IT'S OVERCAST, ONLY 20% MAY HIT THE GROUND.

SIDE ROAD TO ROAD STOP 9
SIDE ROAD TO ROAD STOP 10

Phew! I made it through the atmosphere!

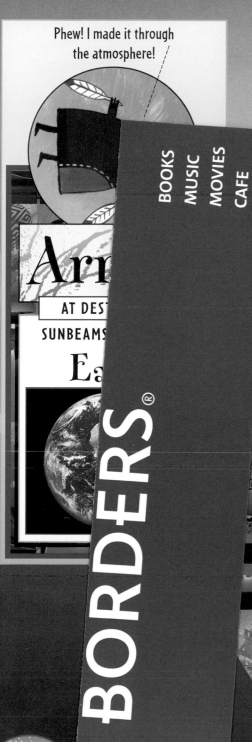
Arr...
AT DEST...
SUNBEAMS...
Ea...

Magic
IN THE ATMOSPHERE

The flares that explode from the surface of the sun thrust very small atomic particles into space at high speeds. When these particles reach the Earth's atmosphere, they collide with gases, making them glow in different colors. From the Earth, this looks like a spectacular light show. This effect is called an **AURORA**.

...OW THE **HIGHWAY** AND DISCOVER HOW PEOPLE SEE THE SUNLIGHT AND FEEL IT. - →

Auroras are only visible near the poles. These are the northern lights, or aurora borealis, which can be seen from the Arctic Circle. The lights seen from Antarctica are called the aurora australis–or southern lights.

SATELLITE
404 miles (650 km) above the Earth

13

Let's go looking for the proof that sunbeams have reached the Earth.

Select
YOUR SIDE ROAD

Sunshine

11 How does sunlight help us see?
(AND WHEN DO WE SEE SUNLIGHT?)

SIDE ROAD TO ROAD STOP 11

12 How do we feel the sun's heat?

SIDE ROAD TO ROAD STOP 12

FOLLOW THE **HIGHWAY**.

Observe!
Experiment with shadows and make a rainbow!

11

How does sunlight help us see?

Objects can only be seen because they reflect the light from something giving out light energy, such as the sun or a light bulb. The reflected light travels from the object to your eyes. Your eyes send a message to the brain.

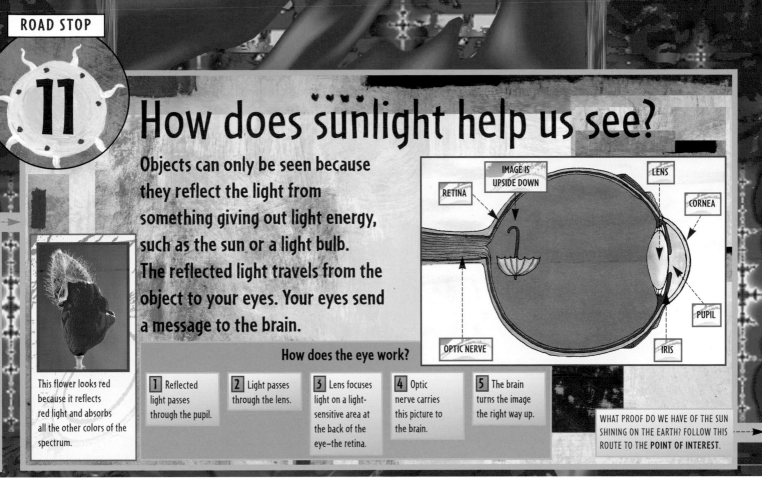

RETINA
IMAGE IS UPSIDE DOWN
LENS
CORNEA
PUPIL
IRIS
OPTIC NERVE

This flower looks red because it reflects red light and absorbs all the other colors of the spectrum.

How does the eye work?

1 Reflected light passes through the pupil.

2 Light passes through the lens.

3 Lens focuses light on a light-sensitive area at the back of the eye—the retina.

4 Optic nerve carries this picture to the brain.

5 The brain turns the image the right way up.

WHAT PROOF DO WE HAVE OF THE SUN SHINING ON THE EARTH? FOLLOW THIS ROUTE TO THE **POINT OF INTEREST**.

FOLLOW THE **HIGHWAY** TO DISCOVER THE EFFECTS OF THE SUN ON THE PLANET AND ITS PEOPLE.

12

How do we feel the sun's heat?

We feel the warmth of the sun in two ways: on our skin and in our blood.

How does your brain react to temperature changes?

The brain is the center of everything you feel and do. It receives signals when your body warms up. You may feel uncomfortable in the heat, so your brain sends messages to your muscles, and you move into the shade.

Detour

LEAP TO **ROAD STOP 18** TO SEE HOW PEOPLE PROTECT THEMSELVES FROM THE SUN'S RAYS.

What happens when your body sweats?

Your body also reacts to the sun's heat without you realizing it. When you get hot, you may sweat, or release a cooling, salty liquid on your skin. As your blood warms up, your body slows down to try to cool down. So your heart may beat slower in hot weather.

Reptiles have a body temperature that changes according to their surroundings. To keep an even temperature, lizards bask in the sunshine at cool times of the day and hide in the shade when the sun is strong.

When do we see sunlight?

To understand the effect that sunlight has on the Earth, we need to examine night and day, shadows, rainbows, and mirages.

Detour

WITHOUT SUNLIGHT THERE WOULD BE NO LIFE ON EARTH. LEAP TO **ROAD STOP 13** TO FIND OUT MORE.

POINT OF INTEREST FROM ROAD STOP 11

1 Night and day

We see sunlight during the day but not at night. This is because the Earth spins on its axis. It goes around once every 24 hours. The side of the Earth that faces the sun has day and the dark side has night. When the sun seems to sink in the sky, it is really the Earth turning away from the sun's light.

Detour

THE SUN HELPS US TELL TIME. LEAP TO **ROAD STOP 20** TO FIND OUT MORE.

FOLLOW THE **HIGHWAY**.

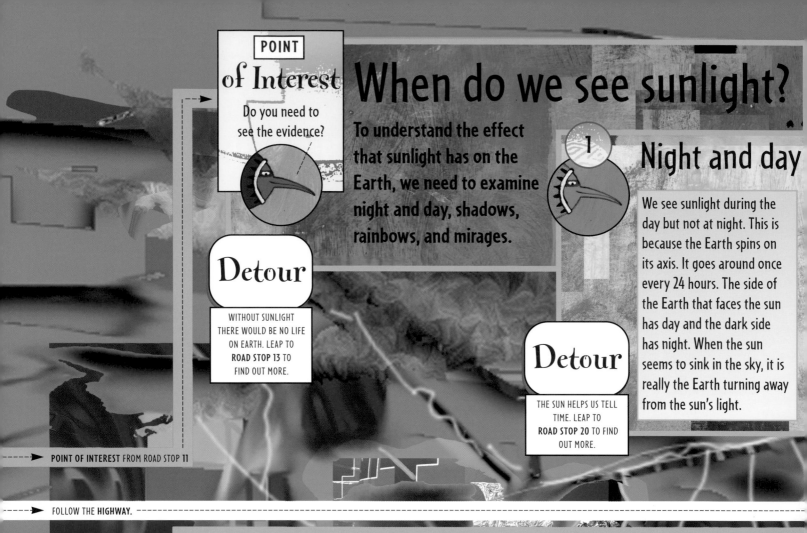

3 Rainbows

If the sun starts to shine while it is raining, you may see a rainbow. The raindrops act like prisms, so that when sunlight shines through them, the light is separated into the colors of the spectrum.

Visible Proof SPOT

Place a mirror at an angle in a plastic dish of water. Stand the dish by a sunny window and wedge a piece of white card between the window ledge and the dish. Watch how the water splits sunlight into the colors of the rainbow.

4 Sunrise and sunset

Although sunlight contains all the colors of the rainbow, at different times of day some of the colors become scattered, and we see those colors that are left behind.

❋ At **SUNRISE** or **SUNSET**, the light has a longer path through the Earth's atmosphere. More of the blue and green rays are scattered in the atmosphere and the sun looks red.

2 Shadows

Light passes through transparent materials, such as glass and water. But many objects are opaque. This means that light cannot pass through them. A shadow falls on the side of the object that the light does not reach.

Opaque objects cast two kinds of shadow: umbra–dark (where no light reaches), and penumbra–gray shadow (where some light reaches).

Visible Proof SPOT

Hold a piece of cardboard directly under a hanging lamp. See the hard and the soft shadows that the cardboard casts.

LIGHT
BOARD
UMBRA
PENUMBRA

SUN — *DAY*

SUN — *NIGHT*

※ Short, strong shadows are formed when the light is very bright and directly overhead.

Detour

ONE MAN WAS SO INTERESTED IN LIGHT AND SHADOW THAT HE SPENT LONG PERIODS OF TIME STUDYING THE SAME SCENE. LEAP TO **ROAD STOP 19**.

※ Soft, long shadows are formed when the sun is low in the sky in the evening.

- - - - - FOLLOW THE **HIGHWAY** AND FIND OUT HOW SUNLIGHT HAS SHAPED OUR PLANET. - - - - - - - - →

5 Mirages

If you are in a car on a hot day, you may see what seems to be a pool of blue water on the road ahead. When you reach that spot, the pool will have disappeared. This vanishing image is called a mirage. It happens because light traveling through the hot air just above the ground tends to ripple, producing an image that appears to be blue water.

※ At **MIDDAY**, the sun is high in the sky. Some of the blue light rays are scattered in the Earth's atmosphere. The sky looks blue and the sun looks yellow.

GREEN FLASH
The sun may flash green for an instant just as it sets. This is because the red rays of light are hidden below the horizon and the blue rays are scattered in the atmosphere. This is very rare!

Without the sun there would be no life on Earth.

Select
YOUR SIDE ROAD

Impact
ON PLANET EARTH

13 How does life depend on the sun?
(AND WHAT IS PHOTOSYNTHESIS?)

14 Can the sun change our landscape?
(HOW ARE SPECIES AFFECTED?)

15 How is the weather affected by the sun?

FOLLOW THE **HIGHWAY.**

SIDE ROAD TO ROAD STOP 13

FOLLOW THE **HIGHWAY.**

SIDE ROAD TO ROAD STOP 13

SIDE ROAD TO ROAD STOP 14

SIDE ROAD TO ROAD STOP 15

※ Today, there are more than 10 million different kinds of creatures on the Earth!

POINT
of Interest

All creatures are part of food chains.

※ Green plants make their own food. They are called producers.

Weather watch!
The sun's energy drives the weather. Look out for swirling winds and blazing bushfires!

Detour

HOW DOES THE SUN AFFECT THE WEATHR? LEAP TO **ROAD STOP 15**.

How does life depend on the sun?

Scientists believe that the first forms of life appeared on the Earth more than 3 billion years ago. The sun's energy is essential to the development of this life.

Living things need the sun's heat and light to survive. Because the Earth is the right distance from the sun, life is possible here. Planets nearer the sun are too hot for life to exist and those farther away are too cold.

The greenhouse effect

1 The atmosphere lets sunlight through, which warms the Earth.

2 Some heat reflects off the atmosphere, back toward the Earth.

3 The Earth heats up more.

※The Earth has a protective layer of air around it called the atmosphere. This stops heat escaping into space, keeping the Earth warm at night when the sun is not shining. The way the Earth's atmosphere can let light in but not let heat out is called the greenhouse effect.

This satellite picture shows the surface of the planet Venus. It has a very thick atmosphere that keeps much of the sun's heat in. The surface is too hot for animals and plants to exist.

Visible Proof SPOT

Next time you go into a greenhouse, notice how warm it is. This is because the glass acts like the atmosphere and lets the sun's heat in but doesn't let all of the heat out.

----- FOLLOW THE **HIGHWAY** TO DISCOVER HOW THE SUN AFFECTS THE WAY PEOPLE LIVE. -----

----- HOW DOES THE SUN SUPPLY FOOD FOR LIVING THINGS? FOLLOW THE PATH TO THE **POINT OF INTEREST**. -----

What is photosynthesis?

This is a process used by green plants to make food by using the sun's energy.

To make food, plants combine carbon dioxide from the air with water from the soil. But they need energy to do this. Chlorophyll, the chemical in plants that makes them green, absorbs light from the sun. This gives plants the energy to drive the food-making process.

CARBON DIOXIDE IN

OXYGEN OUT

CHLOROPHYLL IN LEAVES ABSORBS LIGHT ENERGY

WATER FROM SOIL IN

Visible Proof SPOT

Take three plates and place a damp piece of paper towel on each one. Sprinkle some bean seeds on top of the paper. Now put an upturned glass over one set of seeds and a box with a hole in its side over another. Let the third set grow normally. Keep the paper moist. Bean sprouts grow faster under the glass, because it is warmer. Those under the box lean toward the light coming through the hole. Soon, those plants will need sunlight for healthy growth.

ALL LIVING THINGS ARE PART OF FOOD CHAINS

※ **PLANTS** (producers) use the sun to make food by photosynthesis.

※ **HERBIVORES** (consumers) eat plants.

※ **CARNIVORES** (consumers) eat herbivores or other carnivores.

----- HOW DOES THE SUN CHANGE THE LANDSCAPE AND AFFECT THE SPECIES LIVING ON THE PLANET? **SIDE ROAD** TO ROAD STOP 14 -----

----- HOW DOES THE SUN CHANGE THE WEATHER? **SIDE ROAD** TO ROAD STOP 15 -----

14 Can the sun change our landscape?

The amount of heat that reaches the ground affects the land we live on.

The Earth has a tilted axis. As a result, some parts of the Earth face the sun directly and have summer, and others face it at an angle and have winter. At the equator, the sun's rays strike more directly than anywhere else on the Earth, making it hot. At the poles, the sun's energy is less direct and is spread over a wide area.

IN HOT REGIONS WITH LITTLE RAIN
❋ Strong sunshine dries out the ground making huge cracks appear.
❋ Scorching heat can cause bushfires, especially in very dry areas far away from the coast, such as parts of Australia and the United States.

FOLLOW THE **HIGHWAY.**

15 How is the weather affected by the sun?

It is the sun's energy that drives the weather.

FOLLOW THIS ROUTE TO DISCOVER THE EFFECT OF THE SUN ON THE LANDSCAPE. SIDE ROAD TO ROAD STOP 14

The sun heats water in rivers, lakes, and oceans.

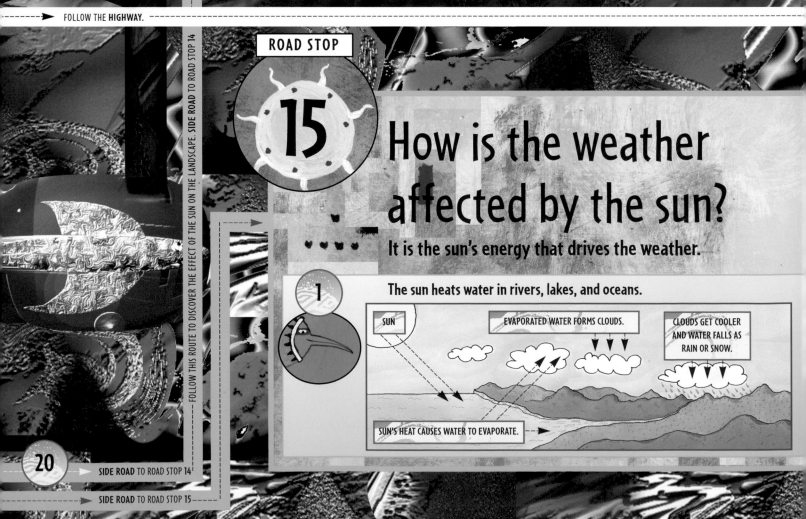

SUN

EVAPORATED WATER FORMS CLOUDS.

CLOUDS GET COOLER AND WATER FALLS AS RAIN OR SNOW.

SUN'S HEAT CAUSES WATER TO EVAPORATE.

SIDE ROAD TO ROAD STOP 14

SIDE ROAD TO ROAD STOP 15

IN COLD, ICY REGIONS

※ Temperatures at the North and South Poles can be as low as -60 °F (-50 °C)!

※ The sun's heat is not warm enough to melt the ice.

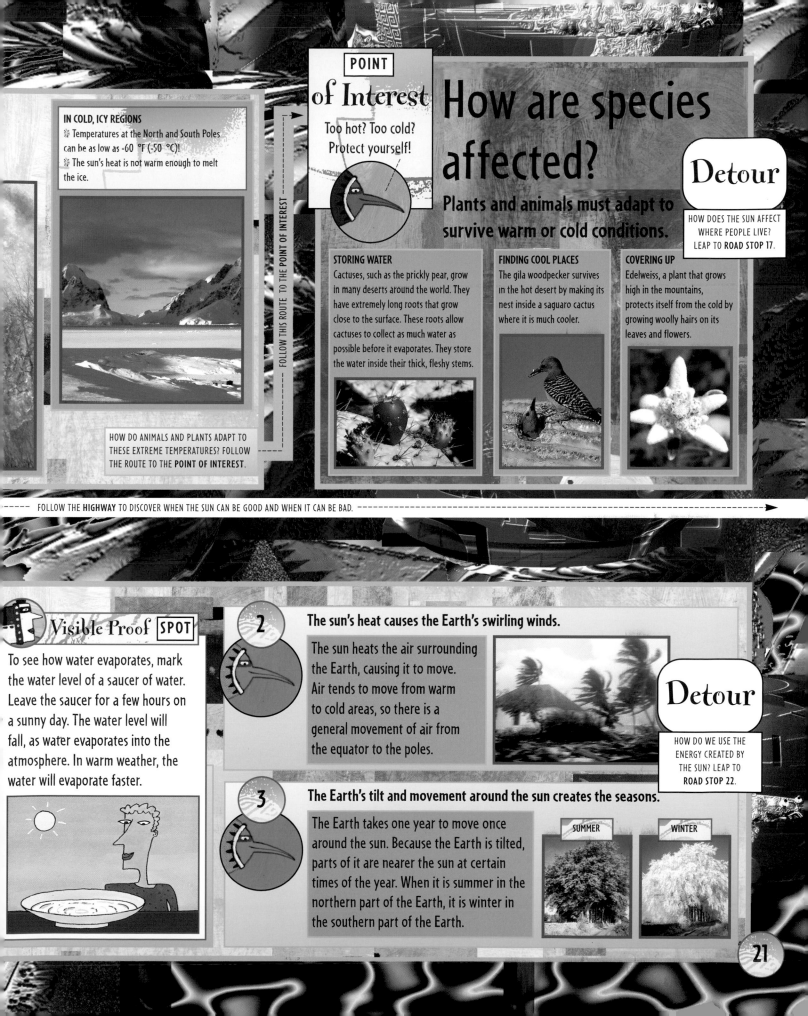

HOW DO ANIMALS AND PLANTS ADAPT TO THESE EXTREME TEMPERATURES? FOLLOW THE ROUTE TO THE **POINT OF INTEREST**.

FOLLOW THIS ROUTE TO THE POINT OF INTEREST

POINT of Interest
Too hot? Too cold? Protect yourself!

How are species affected?

Plants and animals must adapt to survive warm or cold conditions.

Detour

HOW DOES THE SUN AFFECT WHERE PEOPLE LIVE? LEAP TO **ROAD STOP 17**.

STORING WATER
Cactuses, such as the prickly pear, grow in many deserts around the world. They have extremely long roots that grow close to the surface. These roots allow cactuses to collect as much water as possible before it evaporates. They store the water inside their thick, fleshy stems.

FINDING COOL PLACES
The gila woodpecker survives in the hot desert by making its nest inside a saguaro cactus where it is much cooler.

COVERING UP
Edelweiss, a plant that grows high in the mountains, protects itself from the cold by growing woolly hairs on its leaves and flowers.

FOLLOW THE **HIGHWAY** TO DISCOVER WHEN THE SUN CAN BE GOOD AND WHEN IT CAN BE BAD.

Visible Proof [SPOT]

To see how water evaporates, mark the water level of a saucer of water. Leave the saucer for a few hours on a sunny day. The water level will fall, as water evaporates into the atmosphere. In warm weather, the water will evaporate faster.

2 **The sun's heat causes the Earth's swirling winds.**

The sun heats the air surrounding the Earth, causing it to move. Air tends to move from warm to cold areas, so there is a general movement of air from the equator to the poles.

Detour

HOW DO WE USE THE ENERGY CREATED BY THE SUN? LEAP TO **ROAD STOP 22**.

3 **The Earth's tilt and movement around the sun creates the seasons.**

The Earth takes one year to move once around the sun. Because the Earth is tilted, parts of it are nearer the sun at certain times of the year. When it is summer in the northern part of the Earth, it is winter in the southern part of the Earth.

SUMMER WINTER

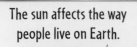

The sun affects the way people live on Earth.

Select

SIDE ROAD TO ROAD STOP 16

SIDE ROAD TO ROAD STOP 17

SIDE ROAD TO ROAD STOP 18

SIDE ROAD TO ROAD STOP 19

FOLLOW THE **HIGHWAY.**

ROAD STOP

16

Is the sun good for people?

The right amount of sun is healthy!

1 **BONES** The body uses sunlight to produce vitamin D, which is essential to the body because it helps you absorb calcium, a mineral that strengthens the bones.

2 **BREATHING** We tend to breathe more deeply and evenly when we sit in the sunshine, and this can help to calm us down.

3 **CIRCULATION** In hot weather, circulation improves as blood vessels open up. Parts of the body then work more efficiently.

4 **HEART** People in tropical countries are less likely to have heart attacks than those in colder areas. Scientists believe that one reason this may be is because they receive more sunshine.

ROAD STOP

17

Does sunlight affect where people live?

Yes. Far fewer people live in areas where temperatures are extreme.

DAYLIGHT OR DARKNESS
Some towns in Greenland, Canada, and Russia are inside the Arctic Circle. In summer months, they have 24 hours of sunlight each day. In the winter, they have days without any sunlight at all.

Some places are simply too hot to live in comfortably and others are too cold. Areas near the North and South poles get very little sunlight during the winter, while countries near the equator are hot all year around.

PEOPLE FIND WAYS TO PROTECT THEMSELVES FROM THE SUN'S HEAT—**SIDE ROAD** TO ROAD STOP **18**

of Interest

This star has the power to cause damage.

Can the sun be bad?

Too much sun can be dangerous.

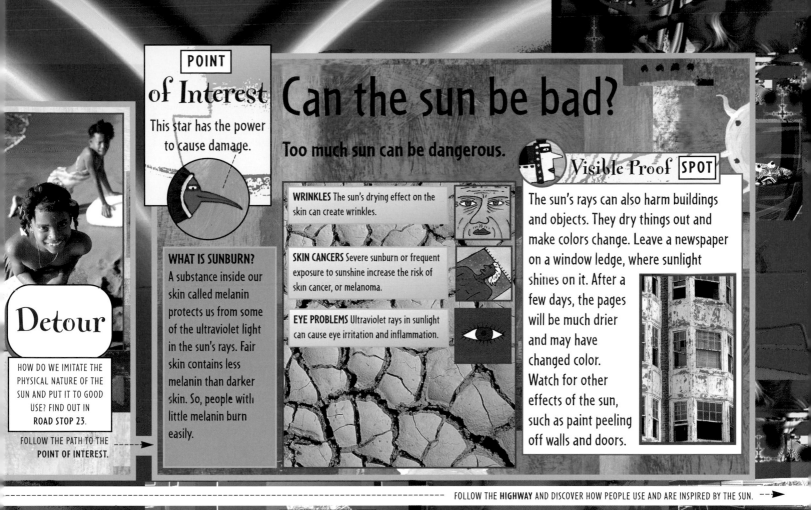

Detour

HOW DO WE IMITATE THE PHYSICAL NATURE OF THE SUN AND PUT IT TO GOOD USE? FIND OUT IN **ROAD STOP 23.**

FOLLOW THE PATH TO THE **POINT OF INTEREST.**

WHAT IS SUNBURN? A substance inside our skin called melanin protects us from some of the ultraviolet light in the sun's rays. Fair skin contains less melanin than darker skin. So, people with little melanin burn easily.

WRINKLES The sun's drying effect on the skin can create wrinkles.

SKIN CANCERS Severe sunburn or frequent exposure to sunshine increase the risk of skin cancer, or melanoma.

EYE PROBLEMS Ultraviolet rays in sunlight can cause eye irritation and inflammation.

Visible Proof SPOT

The sun's rays can also harm buildings and objects. They dry things out and make colors change. Leave a newspaper on a window ledge, where sunlight shines on it. After a few days, the pages will be much drier and may have changed color. Watch for other effects of the sun, such as paint peeling off walls and doors.

FOLLOW THE **HIGHWAY** AND DISCOVER HOW PEOPLE USE AND ARE INSPIRED BY THE SUN.

ROAD STOP

18

How do people protect themselves?

Take a look at these examples.

SAHARA DESERT, AFRICA
* World's largest desert.
* Winter temperature: 50-60 °F (10-16 °C).
* Summer temperature: 86-109 °F (30-43 °C).
* About the same size as the United States but contains more than 250 million fewer people!

ICE CAP, GREENLAND
* Greenland is the world's largest island.
* Winter temperature: about -53 °F (-47 °C).
* Summer temperature: about 12 °F (-11 °C).
* No one lives permanently on the ice cap. People live in areas on the coast that are not as cold.

Some sunscreen lotions protect our skin by blocking out the sun's ultraviolet rays.

In hot countries, buildings may have thick, whitewashed walls to reflect the heat, and small windows to keep out the sun's rays.

In some hot countries, people cover themselves in white clothing. This helps to reflect the heat.

HOW HAVE PEOPLE BEEN MOVED BY THE BEAUTY OF THE SUN? **SIDE ROAD** TO ROAD STOP **19**

19

Are people inspired by the sun?

Artists, writers, and musicians have been moved by the energy, power, and beauty of the sun.

Detour

LEAP TO **ROAD STOP 20** TO SEE HOW SUNLIGHT HELPS US KEEP TRACK OF TIME.

※ **JOSEPH TURNER** (1775-1851), an English artist, made paintings using oil and watercolors that explored the effect of light. He tried to show how bright sunlight colored the sky and the sea. Some of these paintings were so bright and energetic that people criticized his work for not being realistic enough.

The Fighting Temeraire by Turner.

※ The Frenchman **CLAUDE MONET** (1840-1926) explored the way light shines and tried to capture the ever-changing appearance of nature. Monet and his group of painters were named Impressionists after one of Monet's paintings called *Impression–Sunrise* (1870). In his *Haystacks* paintings, he painted the same view of haystacks at different times of the day and with changing weather conditions. He showed how objects seem to change with different amounts of sunlight.

※ **JOSEPH HAYDN** (1732-1809), an Austrian composer, wrote a piece of music called *The Creation* (1798) *that* included a dramatic section in which God makes the sun, bringing light to the Earth.

SIDE ROAD TO ROAD STOP 19

FOLLOW THE **HIGHWAY** TO FIND OUT HOW PEOPLE USE THE SUN.

HOW HAVE PEOPLE WORSHIPED THE SUN? FOLLOW THIS ROUTE TO THE **POINT OF INTEREST**.

FOLLOW THIS ROUTE TO FIND OUT ABOUT THE ARTISTS WHO WERE IMPRESSED BY SUNLIGHT.

POINT of Interest

People worship the giver of life!

How have people worshiped the sun?

In ancient times, people thought of the sun as a god, especially when their survival depended on the heat and light of the sun to grow crops.

Whenever an eclipse occurred, people thought that the sun god was angry with them. They prayed and offered sacrifices to calm down their god.

1 The Inca Indians of South America worshiped the sun, which they called Inti. Inca emperors were believed to have descended from the sun god and were worshiped as divine beings. The Incas sacrificed llamas and guinea pigs in honor of the sun, hoping to ensure a good harvest.

2 The Aztecs of Mexico thought of themselves as "the people of the Sun." Huitzilopochtli was the god of war and the sun. This god shared the main temple with Tlaloc, the rain god, who was important to farmers because drought was always a threat.

3 In the old and middle kingdoms of ancient Egypt (2666-1640 B.C.), people in the Nile Valley worshiped the sun god Re. Egyptians believed that the sun rising and setting was Re sailing a boat across the sky. They built magnificent temples using pyramid and obelisk shapes—symbols of Re.

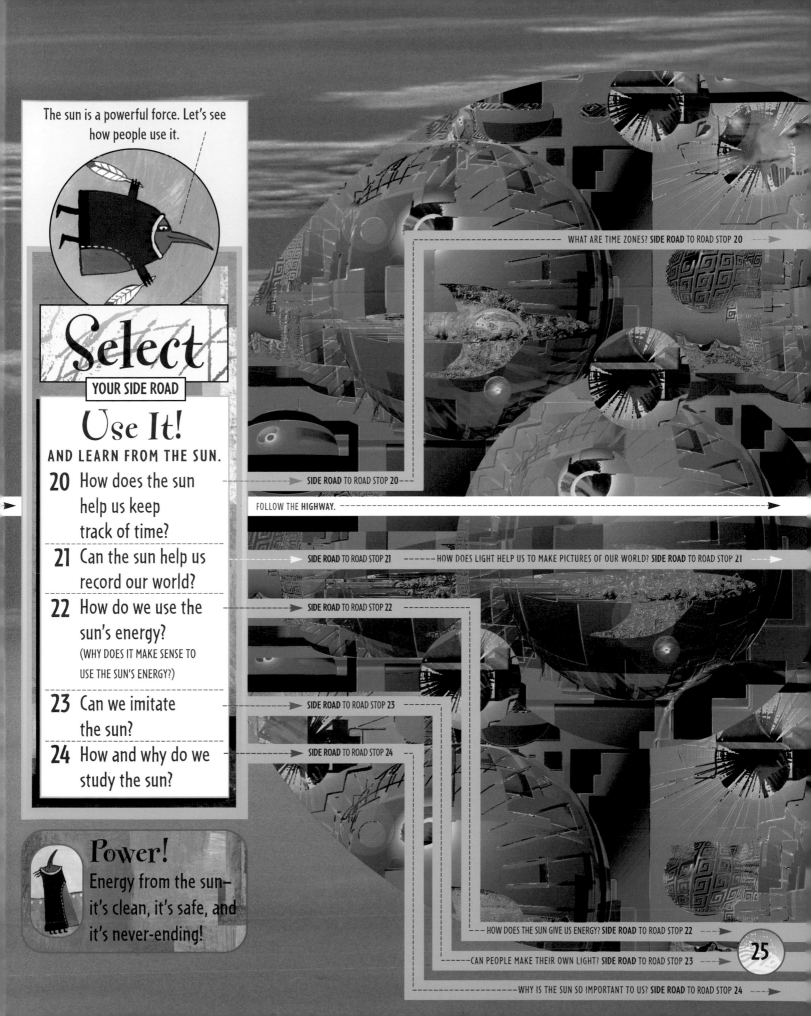

The sun is a powerful force. Let's see how people use it.

Select
YOUR SIDE ROAD

Use It!
AND LEARN FROM THE SUN.

Power!
Energy from the sun—it's clean, it's safe, and it's never-ending!

WHAT ARE TIME ZONES? **SIDE ROAD** TO ROAD STOP 20 ➤

SIDE ROAD TO ROAD STOP 20

FOLLOW THE **HIGHWAY**. ➤

SIDE ROAD TO ROAD STOP 21 HOW DOES LIGHT HELP US TO MAKE PICTURES OF OUR WORLD? **SIDE ROAD** TO ROAD STOP 21 ➤

SIDE ROAD TO ROAD STOP 22

SIDE ROAD TO ROAD STOP 23

SIDE ROAD TO ROAD STOP 24

HOW DOES THE SUN GIVE US ENERGY? **SIDE ROAD** TO ROAD STOP 22 ➤

CAN PEOPLE MAKE THEIR OWN LIGHT? **SIDE ROAD** TO ROAD STOP 23 ➤

WHY IS THE SUN SO IMPORTANT TO US? **SIDE ROAD** TO ROAD STOP 24 ➤

20

How does the sun help us keep track of time?

We use the sun to help us measure time.

SIDE ROAD TO ROAD STOP 20

How did people tell time before they invented clocks?

Ancient peoples made monuments to the sun. Some structures helped them tell the time. The Incas devised a solar calendar, made up of 12 months according to the sun's position in the sky.

This giant sundial, made in Jaipur, India, in 1728, was set up to cast shadows on the ground.

How do sundials work?

Sundials show the time according to where the shadow of a pointer falls. The simplest sundial is a stick in the ground. As the position of the sun changes during the day, the direction of the shadow cast by the pointer also changes.

FOLLOW THE HIGHWAY.

21

SIDE ROAD TO ROAD STOP 21

Can the sun help us record our world?

※ Daguerrotypes were fragile and captured black and white mirror images of the subjects they were recording.

Yes! People have found ways to control light so that it can be used to make pictures of our world.

Who took one of the first photographs?

The Frenchman **LOUIS DAGUERRE** (1787-1851) was one of the first photographers. In 1837, he invented the daguerrotype. This was a piece of metal with a thin surface of light-sensitive chemicals. When this surface was exposed to the sunlight for a few minutes, an image appeared on the metal.

SIDE ROAD TO ROAD STOP 22

SIDE ROAD TO ROAD STOP 23

SIDE ROAD TO ROAD STOP 24

Visible Proof SPOT

See how the sun moves by making a sundial. Cut out a cardboard circle. Glue a triangular piece of cardboard on the circle, as shown. Take your sundial outside and mark a shadow at each hour of the day.

The solar year

WE DIVIDE OUR TIME UP INTO DAYS
ONE DAY = 24 HOURS
THE TIME THE EARTH TAKES TO ROTATE ONCE
MONTHS
ONE MONTH = BASED ON THE TIME TAKEN
FOR THE MOON TO CIRCLE THE EARTH
YEARS
ONE YEAR = THE TIME IT TAKES FOR THE
EARTH TO CIRCLE THE SUN

The phases of the moon

The moon has no light of its own. We can see the moon because it reflects light from the sun. So moonlight is really sunlight reflected off the moon. At different times of the month, the moon appears to be different shapes. These are called the phases of the moon, and the sequence is repeated every 29 days. Our calendar months, which last between 28 and 31 days, are based on the phases of the moon.

Stonehenge in England was probably built to track the movement of the moon and the sun.

What are time zones?

The world is divided into 24 different time zones. As you move eastward into a new time zone, you have to set your watch forward one hour. If you move westward into a new time zone, you have to set your watch backward one hour. Such large countries, as Australia or the United States, contain several different time zones.

WHAT TIME IS IT?

ANCHORAGE
7 P.M.

NEW YORK
3 P.M.

VANCOUVER
6 P.M.

----- FOLLOW THE **HIGHWAY** AND FIND OUT HOW WE USE THE SUN'S ENERGY. -------------------

Visible Proof SPOT

Gather some objects, such as a comb, a feather, and some paper clips. In a room, take a piece of photographic paper out of its box and arrange the objects on top of it. Shine a lamp over the paper for five minutes. When you remove the objects, you will see where they have left their shapes on the paper. Eventually the paper will be dark all over because the light has reached the whole sheet.

Making a photograph

1 When you take a photograph, the light bouncing off the object travels to the film inside the camera.

2 Photographic film has a coating of silver salts that are sensitive to light. When the film is exposed to light, the salts undergo chemical changes. This creates the negative image.

3 To make a photograph, the negative is placed into a projector. Light shines through the negative onto light-sensitive paper. When this paper is treated with chemicals, a photograph is produced.

Detour

PEOPLE CONTINUE TO STUDY SUNLIGHT–WHY? LEAP TO **ROAD STOP** 24.

-- HOW DO WE USE THE SUN'S ENERGY? FOLLOW THIS ROUTE TO ROAD STOP 22 --->

-- HOW DO WE REPLICATE THE SUN'S LIGHT AND ENERGY? FOLLOW THIS ROUTE TO ROAD STOP 23 --->

-- WHAT DO WE HOPE TO LEARN FROM THE SUN? FOLLOW THIS ROUTE TO ROAD STOP 24 --->

27

22

How do we use the sun's energy?

We collect the sun's energy with solar panels. The weather conditions created by the sun's energy can also be used to give us power.

※ The Greek inventor Archimedes, who lived in the 200's B.C., built a giant solar reflector. He called it a *Burning Mirror* and used the reflector to concentrate the sun's rays on enemy warships, causing them to catch fire.

How much energy does the sun provide?
On a sunny day, the energy from the sun that strikes the ground at any point is the same as that given out by a small electric heater. Each day, the amount of solar energy reaching the Earth is thousands of times greater than the energy we make in power stations.

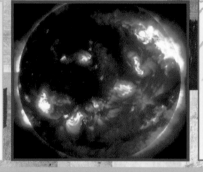

WHAT IS GOOD ABOUT SOLAR POWER? FOLLOW THIS ROUTE TO THE **POINT OF INTEREST**.

POINT of Interest

Solar energy can save us!

Why does it make sense to use the sun's energy?

The sun's energy supply will last for millions of years. This energy is also safe and clean.

These fossils were made from the remains of creatures that lived over 500 million years ago.

Fossil fuels, such as coal, gas, and oil, are formed from tiny plants and animals. When they died millions of years ago, they were buried in mud. Then, over the years, the mud became hard rock and the rotting plants and animals were turned into fossil fuels. It's important that we learn how to use the sun's energy because these fossil fuels may soon run out.

SIDE ROAD TO ROAD STOP 22

SIDE ROAD TO ROAD STOP 23

SIDE ROAD TO ROAD STOP 24

What are solar panels?

These are panels that collect the sun's energy. They are often black, because dark colors absorb more energy than light colors. Sometimes these panels are placed on top of houses. Water passes through the panels in pipes and heats up. The warm water then continues to flow around the house, providing hot water for the home. The panels may turn during the day to follow the path of the sun across the sky.

A greenhouse is a simple way of using the sun's energy. It is used to grow flowers and food and also for drying vegetables so that they can be stored for a long time. The glass lets sunlight in but it does not let much heat escape. This environment allows the plants to grow.

Can we use the weather?

It is the sun's energy that sets the Earth's weather in motion. The energy in the wind and rain is stored solar energy because it is not energy that comes directly from the sun. People can use this energy to create power.

1 WIND POWER

Winds around the world are mainly caused by the sun heating some parts of the Earth more than others. People use the power of wind to turn the sails of windmills, which can generate electricity.

2 HYDROELECTRIC POWER

The sun's heat evaporates water. This makes clouds, and rain falls to make rivers flow. Hydroelectric plants use flowing rivers to turn wheels and make electricity.

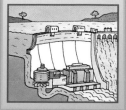

※ Solar energy can be changed into electricity by using panels of solar cells. These cells are made with a material called silicon that gives out electricity when light shines on it.

FOLLOW THIS ROUTE TO THE **POINT OF INTEREST**.

------ FOLLOW THE **HIGHWAY** AND MEET THE PEOPLE WHO HAVE STUDIED THE SUN. ------->

Power that is not safe and clean

When fossil fuels burn, gases are released into the air. Some of these gases, such as sulphur dioxide and nitrogen oxide, dissolve in water drops in the air and make the water acidic. When rain falls, this acidic water can damage trees, soil, and buildings. This is called acid rain.

※ **NUCLEAR POWER** uses the huge amount of energy that is released when the central part of an atom, the nucleus, is split. It causes little pollution–until something goes wrong. In 1986, an explosion at Chernobyl nuclear power station in the former Soviet Union, released a cloud of radioactive gases into the air that contaminated the region's food and water supplies. The remains of the power station are pictured below. The sun is powered by nuclear fusion, in which the nuclei of two or more atoms join together and release energy. If scientists can achieve nuclear fusion on Earth, it could give us a limitless supply of clean, safe power.

Visible Proof SPOT

You can use vinegar, a weak acid, to see how acid rain destroys plants. Dip some leaves in a saucer of vinegar. Then, leave them with their stalks resting in the vinegar for a few days. Soon, the leaves turn brown and die as the acid starts to eat away at them–from both the inside and the outside.

TO FIND OUT ABOUT MAKING ARTIFICIAL LIGHT, FOLLOW THE **SIDE ROAD** TO SHOW ZONE **23**. --->

TO FIND OUT HOW WE USE TELESCOPES TO STUDY THE SUN, FOLLOW THE **SIDE ROAD** TO ROAD STOP **24**.

23

Can we imitate the sun?

Natural light comes from the sun and it cannot be controlled. Artificial light, however, comes from sources that we can control.

Seeing in the dark

People have found ways of imitating the effect of the sun, making light so that they can see even when there is no sunlight. At first, people used fire and candles. Then, they discovered oil and gas and used them to power lamps. Today, electric lights are used throughout the world.

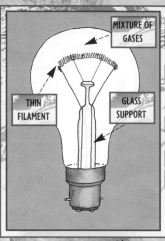

MIXTURE OF GASES

THIN FILAMENT

GLASS SUPPORT

How does an electric light work?

1. Electricity is switched on with a light switch.
2. Electricity flows through a thin coil of tungsten metal called a filament.
3. The filament heats up to more than 9500 °F (2482 °C).
4. It glows white and gives out light.
5. The filament is surrounded by gases other than air. If air could reach the filament, it would burn up.

Neon lights are often used for street signs. They do not have a filament. Instead, they are filled with a gas called neon that produces light when electricity passes through it.

FOLLOW THE **HIGHWAY** TO THE END OF YOUR JOURNEY–A DISTANCE OF 94 ½ MILLION MILES (150 MILLION KILOMETERS).

24

How and why do we study the sun?

We examine the movement and physical nature of the sun because we know that it is crucial for our survival on Earth. The more we know about the "bringer of life" the more we can learn about our world and stars other than the sun.

SUN STUDY TELLS US ABOUT OUR SOLAR SYSTEM AND OTHER STARS.	
DATE	THE ASTRONOMER
AD100?-165?	PTOLEMY OF ANCIENT ALEXANDRIA announced that the Earth was stationary at the center of the universe. He thought that the sun, moon, and the planets all circled the Earth.
1543	NICOLAUS COPERNICUS, a Polish astronomer, stated that the Earth and other planets circled around the sun.
1904	GEORGE ELLERY HALE, an American astronomer, set up the Mount Wilson Observatory in California. This observatory included instruments for studying the sun. Hale realized that by understanding the sun, you could find out about other stars.

※ CORONAGRAPHS photograph the sun's corona, the gases surrounding the sun, by blocking out the light from the photosphere and chromosphere. This is like creating an artificial eclipse.

SIDE ROAD TO ROAD STOP 23

SIDE ROAD TO ROAD STOP 24

Ultraviolet rays

Ultraviolet light is the type of light that can make your skin tan or burn. Overexposure to it can cause skin cancer. The sun is the major source of ultraviolet light, but it can be produced artificially by passing electricity through certain gases.

1 Sun lamps give out ultraviolet light and are used for tanning. People need to be careful under sun lamps because the rays of the sun lamp are much stronger than those of sunlight.

2 Ultraviolet rays can also be used to kill bacteria and viruses. Hospitals use them to sterilize the air and equipment in operating rooms.

※ **LASERS** are instruments that can produce narrow, powerful beams of light. Lasers are precise, safe, and sterile, so they are ideal tools for surgery, especially eye surgery.

How do astronomers study sunlight today?

Astronomers use powerful telescopes to take detailed photographs of sunspots and storms on the sun's surface. The Kitt Peak National Observatory in Arizona has one of the world's largest telescopes. It is positioned on a mountain about 6,875 feet (2,096 m) high. Because it is above the clouds, there is less water vapor to look through. Such vapor sometimes makes it difficult to see a clear image of the sun's surface.

HOW DOES IT WORK?

At the top of a tower there is a flat mirror, 158 in. (4 m) wide. It turns and follows the sun. This mirror bounces the sunlight to a curved mirror 492 ft. (150 m) below the ground, which reflects the sunlight on another mirror. This last mirror projects the sun's image into a viewing room. The final image is nearly 3 ft. (1 m) wide.

※ **SKYLAB**, the first space station, was launched in 1973. Telescopes on board measured different types of radiation from the sun.

From the source—
sun
to the destination—
Earth

A journey that happens everyday, bringing heat, light, and energy to a planet that would otherwise be a barren rock orbiting around in the universe.

Imagine!
Is the sun the only star giving life to a planet, or is there life elsewhere in another galaxy?

Invisible Journeys

Sun

Index

※ PICTURE CREDITS Front cover: left, right: Science Photo Library; center: Pictor. Back cover: Science Photo Library. Inside: P1 background: Pictor. P3 top: Science Photo Library; bottom: Werner Forman Archive/Egyptian Museum, Cairo. P5 NASA/Science Photo Library. P6 NASA/Science Photo Library. P7 top, bottom: NASA/Science Photo Library. P8 background: Pictor; top: Science Photo Library. P9 background: Pictor; top, bottom: Science Photo Library. P10 top left, bottom: Pictor; top right: Science Museum/Science & Society. P11 Science Photo Library. P12 background: Pictor. P13 background: Pictor; left, right: Science Photo Library. P15 top: Science Photo Library; bottom left: Tony Stone; bottom right: Pictor. P16 left: Science Photo Library; right: Pictor. P17 top right, center right: Tony Stone; bottom right: Science Photo Library; bottom left: Pictor. P18 bottom: Pictor; top: Tony Stone. P19 top: NASA/Science Photo Library. p20 Science Photo Library. P21 top left, center right: Pictor; top center left: Planet Earth Pictures; top center right, top right: Oxford Scientific Films; bottom left, bottom right: Science Photo Library. P22 Tony Stone. P23 top left, bottom left: Tony Stone; top center: Science Photo Library; top right, bottom center, bottom right: Pictor. P24 background: Pictor; top: Bridgeman Art Library/National Gallery London; bottom right; Bridgeman Art Library/British Museum; bottom left: Mary Evans; P25 background: Pictor. P26 bottom: Werner Forman Archive; p27 top right: Science Photo Library; top left: Pictor. P28 top, bottom: Science Photo Library. P29 top left: Pictor; top right: Eye Ubiquitous; bottom left, bottom right: Science Photo Library. P30 Pictor. P31 top left, top right: Science Photo Library; bottom right: Pictor.